UNLESS YOU BECOME LIKE THIS CHILD

HANS URS VON BALTHASAR

UNLESS YOU BECOME LIKE THIS CHILD

Translated by
ERASMO LEIVA-MERIKAKIS

IGNATIUS PRESS   SAN FRANCISCO

Title of the German original:
Wenn ihr nicht werdet wie dieses Kind
© 1988, Schwabenverlag AG
Ostfildern / Stuttgart

Cover design by Roxanne Mei Lum
Cover art: *Christ among the Children*
Emil Nolde (1910)
Oil on canvas, 34⅛ x 41⅞″
Collection, The Museum of Modern Art, New York
Gift of Dr. W. R. Valentiner
Photograph © 1991, The Museum of Modern Art, New York

© 1991, Ignatius Press, San Francisco
ISBN 978-0-89870-379-5
Library of Congress catalogue number 91-73329
Printed in the United States of America

CONTENTS

"To be childlike: That is best of all. Nothing is more difficult than bearing one's own weakness. God helps with everything."

—*Novalis, shortly before his death*

"O, would that I were as children are!"

—*Hölderlin, already demented*

I

GOD'S KINGDOM IS FOR CHILDREN

JESUS' ATTITUDE TOWARD CHILDREN is perfectly clear. No one will enter the Kingdom of God, which has come close to us in Jesus, unless he makes a turnabout and returns to the mentality of his beginnings. "Amen I say to you: Whoever does not receive the Kingdom of God like a child will not enter into it" (Mk 10:15). But how should someone already well on the way into his future life suddenly stop and set out in the opposite direction? asks the Jewish alderman in wonderment. However, Jesus is even more amazed by this question: "You pretend to be a teacher in Israel and do not know this?" (Jn 3:10). He assumes this is something elementary, the condition for everything else! "Can someone, then, return to his mother's womb and be born again?" Pure thought seems to prove the absurdity of such a contention. But Jesus does not himself find it the least bit absurd: being the grown man he is, he has none-theless never left the "Father's bosom". Even now, having become man, he "dwells" in the Father (Jn 1:18) and only as one dwelling in the Father can he reveal anything valid about him.

We are confronted at one moment with a child chosen in the street, a child which the disciples want to keep away from Jesus as being insignifi-cant and bothersome. To this Jesus objects: "Let the children come to me and do not hinder them" (Mt 19:14). And suddenly we take a leap from this child to the unique child that Jesus himself is. And Jesus does not see in this any leap over an abyss but, on the contrary, a direct continuity, for "whoever welcomes such a child in my name, welcomes me" (Mt 18:5). A child, therefore, is not merely a distant analogy for the Son of God: whoever turns with loving concern "to such a child" (any one out of hundreds of thousands), and does this, consciously or unconsciously, in the name of Jesus, of one mind with him—that person is welcoming the archetypical Child who has his abode in the Father's bosom. And because this Child cannot be separated from his abode, whoever turns to the most insignificant of children is, in fact, attaining to the ultimate, to the Father himself: "Whoever welcomes me is not welcom-ing me but him who sent me" (Mk 9:27). In the context of the Gospel, however, what is intended here is not a form of social welfare but a profound mystery, rooted in the very being of Christ, whose identity is inseparable from his being a child in the bosom of the Father. The mystery of Christ is inseparable as well from what was said at the outset concerning the interior turning in the direction of spiritual childhood, toward what Jesus calls "birth from the spirit" or "rebirth from above" or, simply, "birth from God" (Jn 1:13). This is what he repeatedly stresses as being the express condition for entering into the Kingdom of God: "Whoever is not born again cannot see the Kingdom of God", "cannot enter into the Kingdom of God" (Jn 3:3, 5).

And yet, at first sight, what is involved is something wholly understandable for us, an experience that each of us has had as a child and to which we must somehow return, an experience which every adult can approximate in his dealings with children, especially children of his own. Jesus does not seek out a "model child" in order to hold him up as an example. Things are much simpler: "Then he took a child, placed him in their midst, put his arms about him and spoke to them" (Mk 9:36f.). What he wants to show with the child he is lovingly embracing is something very simple, which the listening disciples should be able to understand as easily as the meaning of a straightforward parable. And yet, because Jesus is embracing the child as he speaks, his simple words acquire an unexpected, still undetected significance. The Jews,

along with the Greeks and Romans, saw childhood as a stage on the way to fullness of humanity.
It occurred to no one to consider the distinctive
consciousness of children as a value in itself. And,
because childhood was ranked as merely a "not-
yet" stage, no one was concerned with the form
of the human spirit, indeed the form of man's
total spiritual-corporeal existence, that preceded
free, moral decision-making. But obviously, for
Jesus, the condition of early childhood is by no
means a matter of moral indifference and insignifi-
cance. Rather, the ways of the child, long since
sealed off for the adult, open up an original dimension in which everything unfolds within the
bounds of the right, the true, the good, in a zone
of hidden containment which cannot be derogated
as "pre-ethical" or "unconscious", as if the child's
spirit had not yet awakened or were still at the
animal level—something it never was, not even
in the mother's womb. That zone or dimension
in which the child lives, on the contrary, reveals
itself as a sphere of original wholeness and health,
and it may be even said to contain an element of
holiness, since at first the child cannot yet distinguish between parental and divine love.

Jesus naturally knows how deeply exposed to
danger this originally inviolable dimension is.
Childhood is fully vulnerable because the child is
powerless, while those who care for him enjoy
an all-powerful freedom. Instead of leading him

rightly they can lead him astray in a variety of egotistical ways, oftentimes in a manner which is quite unconscious of its moral indifference. Hence Jesus' terrible threat to such a seducer: "It would be better for him to be thrown into the sea with a millstone round his neck than to lead one of these little ones astray" (Lk 17:2).

Jesus also knows that the fragility of this originally inviolable dimension can—because of original sin and the abiding propensity to temptation—lead to definitive breaks when a young person enters the age when he must decide for or against evil. The "supra-moral" rightness and goodness of the original dimension must now be affirmed with fullness of freedom. But, for those who set themselves self-consciously apart from that dimension, its goodness and truth must now appear to be only one of the possibilities of goodness and truth, which thereby assume the visage of the general, the abstract, the juridical. It is precisely such a crossroads, such a being-placed before the good as a "law" (of God or of society) to be chosen, that in conclusion appears to both Jews and Gentiles as the ideal situation for one to be confirmed in adult morality.

Again, Jesus knows that this process of growing out of an originally protected condition is the unavoidable path man must follow. But what he envisages is an integration of the "supra-moral", holy treasures of our original condition into the time of our maturity. Paul expresses Jesus' expectations correctly when he says: "Brothers, do not be childish in your outlook. Be as innocent of evil as babes but become adults in your thinking" (1 Cor 14:20). How can these apparent incompatibles be made compatible? Only in this way: if the apparently abstract law is put by God in a childlike heart so that it becomes as concrete as it was originally (Jer 31:33). This can occur only if God deposits his own Spirit within our heart ("I will put my Spirit within you", Ez 36:27), a Spirit which does not make us childish but can gather up in our heart and utter forth the cry of "Abba, Father!" This is what it means to receive from God the *instinctus Spiritus Sancti*, as Thomas Aquinas calls the gift grace gives the human heart for it to be able to respond to God's movement of love. Such an adult, who has also recovered at a higher level the concrete spontaneity of the child, is called by Novalis "the synthetic child".

2

THE HUMAN CHILD

WHAT IS JESUS POINTING TO when he insists that the attitude of the human child is necessary for salvation, for entering the Kingdom of God? We must not idealize each person's childhood as a (lost) paradise or ascribe to the child virtues which he does not and cannot have, simply because he lives before the stage of the conscious and free "acquisition" of virtuous attitudes. Nevertheless, there does exist a sphere in which every person born possesses an archetypical model in keeping with which he is to direct his conscious life, surely following the course of his existence into the future but always with the memory of his origins before him. The end-form, the Omega, toward which his life is moving cannot be other than the original form, the Alpha, out of which he lives and which provides him the very instruments for his striving.

Between the mother and the child she bears in her womb there exists an "archetypical identity", a unity which by no means is purely "natural", "physiological" or "unconscious": the child is already itself, is already something "other" than the mother because it derives from the man's seed as much as from her. She had to conceive in order for the child to come to be in her, to come out of her most intimate being, as of course the father too had to receive from his wife in order to become fruitful in her. They had to be "two in one flesh", with mutual gratitude, in order to be able to procreate in love the new life that surpasses them both, the new life that will owe its existence to both of them together but for which they, together, will always have to be thankful in the sight of the absolute creative Power that transcends them: "Children are a gift of the Lord" (Ps 127:3). Neither father nor mother would pretend that their contribution has given the child its spirit, its freedom, its immediacy with God.

Behind the "archetypical identity" of mother and child, moreover, there emerges an even deeper "archetypical identity" based on their non-identity, which at birth makes itself plain to all. I speak of the "identity" between the child, an existing and developing reality, and the idea that God has of him, the intention therefore that God wishes to realize with him. This idea and intention is God himself and yet not, in so far as it has the creature for an object. It is precisely on the basis of this even more fundamental "archetypical identity" that we can demonstrate what is specifically Christian in the new, post-Classical manner of evaluating childhood: in Christ, for the first time, we see that in God himself there exists—within his inseparable unity—the distinction between the Father who gives and the Gift which is given (the Son), but only in the unity of the Holy Spirit.

One reflection of this primal Christian mystery, source of all other mysteries, is the fact that, within the endangerment and fragility of human existence, the unity between mother and child can prevail even in their separation. The child at its mother's breast is, first of all, something of a repetition of their bond while in the womb. And yet this unity in love persists even when the mother's face smiles at the child at a distance. Here is where the miracle occurs that one day the child will recognize in its mother's face her protective love and will reciprocate this love with a first smile. Before making any judgment or coming to any conclusion, we must marvel as at a miracle at the perfect and immediate intuition which is here operative. Love is understood to be the most pristine source of all. This understanding opens up in the child the dormant bud of self-awareness. The love between a thou and an I inaugurates the reality of a world which is deeper than simple being because of its absolute boundlessness and plenitude. And, since this opening up occurs on the basis of love, unbounded being is seen to be the reality that makes sense, that is self-evidently right: in short, the truth which is identical with the good. We call this an "intuition" and not a discursive process of reasoning because the mother's smile is not interpreted as love subsequently; it is intuition, too, because in the awakening spirit the understanding of being as such is always awaiting the moment of realization, and this precisely in the concrete event that is offered through ever-open, ever-watchful senses.

Although it derives from a concrete encounter and thus does not at all communicate an abstract concept of being, this intuition is wholly unbounded and reaches to the Ultimate, to the Divine. This is why, for a child, his parents' concrete love is not at first separable from God; if everything follows an even course, this difference must be tenderly shown him by his parents' humility and their own dependency on God. If this occurs as it should, the "archetypical identity" will once again be confirmed for him in expanded form. The child will see clearly that love is realized only in reciprocity, in an oppositeness that is encounter and not opposition, a relationship that is held together in its very difference by the spirit of love and that, far from being endangered by mutuality, is rather strengthened by it. Love, too, is what enables the child to experience its absolute neediness as something other than a threat, since it is lived as the situation in which the mother's ever-latent love may be realized always anew.

The "archetypical identity", which we discover in creatures within a clear separation of persons who are held together by love, is a creaturely *imago trinitatis*, veiled and yet not wholly invisible. Jesus points to this final aspect when he says that the angels of these little ones "are always contemplating the face of my Father" (Mt 18:10), as if they were the living representatives of their idea in God. For this opening up to perdure to the ultimate, the transparency of the *imago trinitatis* among father, mother and child must be as perfect as possible. Any disturbance the child begins to sense—whether between the parents or one parent and the child—confuses and clouds over the horizon of absolute being and, therefore, also its bestowal of all creaturely being as a gift of God. Such a vision becomes troubled, too, because the child can grasp the gift of all existence only within the concreteness of its relationship of love with its parents within the peaceful realm of the familiar space it inhabits. Any violence in this realm of wholeness inflicts wounds in the child's heart which for the most part will never heal. Those who always bear the burden of suffering in the case of a divorce, and very often in the problems resulting from marriages between members of different faiths, are the children. Only seldom do adults realize what immeasurable harm they thus inflict on children, and how close they come as a result to the most terrible of Jesus' curses: "Whoever is a cause of stumbling to one of these little ones who believe in me . . . " (Mt 18:6).

To say this already implies how threatened interiorly the originally wholesome world of the child is. The mother is not always there, often even in moments when the child thinks it cannot do without her. The feeling of being sheltered, which can span wide distances, is nonetheless threatened from within by a fear that a life of love could die: this is a fear that can penetrate to the very bottom of the heart, as with a child who, in the middle of the whirlwind of urban traffic, suddenly feels helplessly abandoned. As long as it feels borne along by a tide of sheltering care, the child is sure of having an open refuge; but within this security it can begin to realize that the care with which its mother and others surround it costs effort and self-sacrifice. The child thus becomes more aware, on the one hand, of the fact that such loving care is a gift; but, on the other hand, it also begins to discern the hardships that govern the earthly scene.

The child sees that its parents are obeying a duty when they assume the responsibility of caring for it. Especially in the case of the mother, but also of the father, this duty is contained within the original sphere of the concrete good, in which they are bound up with the child. They live out an obedience to the laws of existence that is inextricably united with fatherhood and motherhood. But there is also involved a part of free willingness that has to be achieved through personal decision. Here we encounter a paradox which in the end can be resolved only at a supernatural and Christian level. For, in his helplessness, the child has a sacred right to be cared for; but only love can do justice to such a right. Thus, the child has a right to something that transcends the juridical dimension and which can be satisfied only out of a free initiative and gift of self. In the beginning the child cannot distinguish between absolute goodness, which is divine, and the creaturely goodness he encounters in his parents. Consequently, this right to goodness is a sacred right whose satisfaction can occur only on the basis of a most intimate bond between the parents and the mind of God. Now, once God has placed a creature in existence, his divine response to his creature's entreaty is infallibly a unity of "duty" and free love bestowed as a grace. The Holy Spirit cannot be refused to one who cries "Abba, Father!" (Lk 11:13).

The Gospel takes it for granted that even loveless men ("you who are evil", Lk 11:13) cannot remain closed to the loving entreaty of a child. Since evil is nevertheless present, however, the loving answer to a rightful entreaty stands in danger.

So it is with all other attributes native to children: all of them are modeled on the wholesome exchange of love between the primarily giving love of the mother and the primarily received love of the child. For the child it is natural to receive good gifts, and so docility, obedience, trust and sweet surrender are not for him virtues to be expressly achieved but the most unreflectedly natural things in the world. This is so to such an extent that the child adopts the mother's giving attitude unquestioningly as the right one, and he gives spontaneously when he has something to give. He shows his little treasures without hiding any of them; he wants to share because he has experienced sharing as a form of goodness. The fact that he can make this attitude his own presupposes that he does not need to distinguish between the giver and the gift, since both at the mother's breast and in all other things given him the two are one: in the gift the child directly recognizes the love of the giver. It is the expressly perceivable egotism of the giver ("you who are evil") that results in the gift's no longer being understood as the image of the giver: only then does the inclination to private possession become split in the child from its use as possible gift. Then we see vanish the spontaneous seeking of refuge in the place of protection and obedience as the immediate response to the "fostering" source; only then does concrete "fosterance" (*auctoritas*, from *augere*: "to make grow", "to foster") become abstract, legal "authority".

Here arises the burning question whether the ruling, concrete authority of the parents in the family in regard to the children is something preliminary which is then enhanced to the seemingly all-encompassing and definitive authority of the state or of society, whose element of fostering care replaces that of the family. In his philosophy of law, Hegel is convinced of the necessity of such a disjuncture: to the family he attributes only a "naturally ethical spirit" of "love" as a kind of "stimulus"; but this spirit must then develop into an autonomous, self-determined spirit, something possible only within the greater unity of the state and on condition of a separation from the endangering source which enables the second phase of the spirit "to triumph". But the fourth commandment of the Mosaic decalogue stands opposed to this confiscation of the individual by the state, and it is a commandment that Christ reaffirms and which enjoins on adults, too, the respectful love of children for parents. Even when the educational element of the parents' authority disappears as the children come of age, this does not abolish the original relationship of giving and responding personal love between children and parents. This relationship only acquires a new accent which imposes on the children the care for aging parents as a permanent and loving duty of responsive gratitude: after all, children owe their physical existence to their parents, and this is a debt which can never be adequately paid. In this sense, so much remains vivid of the original relationship in the general memory of mankind that this duty out of gratitude on the part of children cannot simply vanish into thin air, as in the case of animals once they abandon the nest. Even beyond a purely juridical rationale, we may affirm that in man a fragment remains intact of the original "archetypical identity in the distinction between mother and child", as an element of a love that transcends juridical considerations even as it contains them.

This proves to be relevant when children grow up and themselves become mothers and fathers. Even though in this case they will have an active experience of "archetypical identity", still they will not quite be able to dissociate it from the passive form of it they had once experienced. The experience immerses them in the great stream of memory of generations whom they cannot cease to thank for their existence and whose past becomes for them the present, to the extent that, along with their progeny, they look out toward the future. The reciprocity with which both the past and the future point to the present is, once again, a fragment of archetypical childhood, in which a confident and

24

trusting expectation of the good has its basis in the experience of already having received it.

As precarious as this time-structure is within the sphere of a guilty human race (again we think of "you who are evil . . ."), in that same measure is it fully realized in the new childhood intended by Jesus in a relationship with the perfect and all-good Father. For here the confident hope in the good things asked for becomes so infallible on the basis of the goodness that has already been experienced that this hope, even as such, becomes a present reality: "Whatever you ask for and pray for, believe that you have already received it and it will be yours" (Mk 11:24). "We can approach God with joyful confidence for this reason: if we make requests which accord with his will he listens to us; and if we know that all our requests are heard by him, we know also that we already possess the things we ask him for" (1 Jn 5:14–15).

3

THE CHILD OF GOD AND MAN

EVERYTHING WE HAVE SAID HERE concerning the human child belongs to human nature and, therefore, is not really the object of God's revelation of himself in Jesus Christ. Nevertheless, man's alienation from God has so buried in oblivion so many of man's own deepest aspects that these can be brought up again into the light of memory and human self-understanding only through God's Incarnation. For our present concerns, this occurs when Jesus stresses the indispensable character of a truly childlike mentality in order to participate in the Kingdom of God which he has brought near. This demands of Jesus' listener a reawakening to his true origin, to which he has turned his back, a spiritual turnabout ("unless you convert and become like children") that will enable him to become aware of himself. And since this turning about takes place in obedience to Jesus, it must count on the illuminating light of his grace if it is to succeed. The contours of what we tried to describe in the preceding chapter will now become delineated under the rays of this light.

In this connection we must wonder why Jesus does not speak of his own experience of child-hood—a childhood that must have had a modality all its own since he was no ordinary child, but the eternal Son of the Father become man. Thick veils cover his childhood: with the sole exception of the episode of the twelve-year-old Jesus at the temple, the infancy narratives tell us nothing concerning the child himself. This one episode, however, does cast a bright light back on his darkly hidden early years.

Before we go on to consider this, however, we must remember one overarching fact: Jesus speaks with such familiarity about the child's specific manner of being and dignity that such knowledge must be rooted in his own experience. This experience of childhood, further, has remained, in the case of Jesus, a deeper and more authentic dimension of consciousness than can be said of any philosopher or founder of a religion, or of any psychologist who attempts to re-live by empathy the phase of childhood. And, when Jesus points to the child, he is bringing out the religious dimension in all those things we have discussed: identity within separation, unity and difference of giver and gift, receptiveness out of need, but all of it in the richness of love, gratitude, recourse, protectedness, obedience. In so doing, however, Jesus is not importing foreign elements into the child's existence; he is but bringing to light one element that traverses all other aspects and that provides them with their most basic foundation.

His doing this, his being able to do it, rests on the uniqueness of his experience of childhood. He has no need to demonstrate in his own case what there is in this experience that equally applies to all men; he leaves that to the meditation of his believers, who have given expression to such a contemplation in hundreds of thousands of pictures representing Mother and Child. The variety of such portrayals is great: Child being suckled at the Mother's breast, or sleeping on her, or playing with his Mother, or taking some gift from her (a fruit or a flower), or embracing her or busying himself from her protective lap as from a throne with something coming toward him: the treasure of the Three Kings or his little cousin John. The scene can be portrayed in a more strictly religious or in a more secularized form—even the stark icons do not disdain the representation of human tenderness—but everywhere what is being indicated is the fact of the authentic status as a child of him who "became like us in all things except sin" (Heb 4:15).

Nonetheless, Jesus' experience of childhood must have been unique. For it is the eternal Son of God who becomes man, and his eternal and loving readiness to execute every saving plan of the triune God becomes concretized, through the Holy Spirit, in one individual human child. It is beyond the realm of possibility that this Child suddenly becomes aware at some point along his development that he is the Son of God and, therefore, himself God. Thus, even his earliest consciousness, though perhaps in a quite implicit mode, must have known his being embraced in the bosom of the infinite and personal Father. The Child Jesus reposed in his Mother's womb in "archetypical identity" and came forth from it to have the experience of every human child as a result of Mary's turning in love toward him—the experience of being two in one, one with the Mother in her love and separate from her: such a union of love presupposes the otherness of each of the two loving parties. And we have shown how the horizon of all being opens up for the child in precisely this primal experience. But in the Child Jesus this experience, the basis for all that is properly human, must have been a direct transparency of his experience of being at home in the bosom of his Divine Father: separate from him as the Son, receiving his being as Son from the Father, but within this separation inseparably united in their common Holy Spirit.

We showed, however, how in the human child this primal experience is shot through with an anguishing intimation of a deeper, more dangerous separation: the mother can be absent when needed; the child can experience what it would be like to be left alone. . . . Now, in the Child Jesus the mission which becomes incarnate is an indivisible whole which from the outset contains its conclusion: abandonment by God. In no way does this Child's attitude anticipate an express knowledge about the impending Cross; but his trusting obedience to the Father includes the readiness to go as far as the Father's loving will may dispose. This primal trust in the Father, which no mistrust ever clouds, rests on the Holy Spirit common to Father and Son. In the Son, the Spirit keeps alive the unshakable trust that the Father's every ordinance (even the transformation of the distinction of persons into abandonment) will always be an ordinance of love, which the Son, now that he is a man, must reciprocate with human obedience.

But how, in this Child, can the primal experience of being at home in the Mother's bosom, so to speak, "double up" in the simultaneous primal experience of being at home in the bosom of the eternal Father? An initial answer would be that, in the depths of this Child's soul, there slumbers the awareness of being the divine Son, and that, when the Mother awakens him, the opening up of the whole horizon of reality is experienced not only as something holy but as the realization that in the depths of this opened fullness of being there radiates the personal Face of his Father, personally turned toward him. But this answer does not yet suffice fully to clarify this mystery. We must likewise consider that the Virgin Mother knows about the Child's direct origin in God, and that, even in her first embrace of love, she is a living reminder of the ultimate mystery of the Child's belonging in the bosom of the Father. An ordinary child distinguishes relatively late between parental and divine love; but, in the Child Jesus, this distinction, even quite implicitly, must have been active from the first moment of human consciousness. However, this does not mean a depreciation of the unity of Mother and Child, only that such union is sensed from the beginning to be a gift of the Father in the Holy Spirit who has overshadowed the Mother.

And, since the handmaid of the Lord had made herself available from the outset in an attitude of perfect obedience, we must presume that in her, too, inarticulately perhaps, there was present the will to give back to God what he had given her, just as Abraham was ready to restore to God the son of the promise God had bestowed. It will not be long before she hears the words, "And your own heart a sword shall pierce", which transform her basic readiness to renounce into an event hidden in the future. Neither the Son nor the Mother necessarily had to possess, ahead of time, a definite idea of the Cross and the abandonment by God, events which will involve the Mother: "Behold your son there!" But the assent of each to total separation as the sealing off of the original unity was present from the outset.

Most persons have an experience of sin in the world rather early on, and their memory of the concrete experience of their source goes underground. The open horizon of reality becomes filled with all manner of figures that are held together by the concepts "being" and "reality", which have now become abstract. Such thinking and judging in the abstract serve them as a sign of autonomy and maturity. For Jesus, however, the ground that permeates and unifies everything in his life remains always identical with the concrete and personal reality of the Father, so that he can define himself by speaking about "my Father". Precisely this shows to what extent he remains a child even as an adult, and why this permanent characteristic gave him such a unique understanding of childhood and made him exalt so highly the condition of being a child. We will leave for later the question of how Jesus can expect us, guilty humans that we are, to recover this precious treasure we have lost.

We must first of all examine the truth that the Child Jesus, like every human child, must have undergone a process of maturing to the point of full adulthood. In no way is it surprising that he required thirty years to attain to full maturity of his mission, particularly in the case of such an incomparable mission. We are not in a position to describe the stages of his ever deeper initiation into his divine and human task: these lie deeply hidden in his prayer, in his interior surrender to the Father who reveals himself to him ever more profoundly, and also in the increasing ability of his human nature to comprehend as it blossoms at all levels. We must allow this process all the time it requires. The words of the twelve-year-old Jesus, "Did you not know that I must be about my Father's business?", should not lead us to conclude that here Jesus is already expressing a fully mature consciousness of his mission. To be sure, the essential part of his mission, which has been present in his awareness from the outset, can indeed be seen as formulated in this statement of the boy: the truth that, even as one who has been sent out, he never ceases to repose in the bosom and will of the Father. Indeed, this essential fact already surpasses the understanding of his parents. Nevertheless, such a consciousness of his mission remains consonant with his age. Full maturity first becomes apparent at the event of the baptism, when the Father speaks the word that sends the Son forth into his public ministry and when the Father as well sends the Son the Holy

Spirit as necessary for the actual accomplishment of this mission.

It may be difficult for us to bring both things into harmony: on the one hand, the presence, from the beginning, of the full mission in the small Child, who can envision it in its totality in a genuine, even if childlike, manner; on the other hand, the human process of maturing and the ever deeper understanding of this totality, until the total mission has attained, within the adult human consciousness, the plenitude that will allow its autonomous and responsible execution. Actually, it is at this final point that the real difficulty begins. How can the assumption of full, personal responsibility for what one does and decides to do be reconcilable with the abiding childlike attitude toward the Father that makes Jesus say in John's Gospel: "The Son can do nothing on his own initiative; he does only what he sees the Father doing" (Jn 5:19)? "He who sent me is present with me, and has not left me alone; for I always do what is pleasing to him" (8:29). "Whoever believes in me, believes not in me but in him who sent me . . . for I do not speak on my own authority" (12:44, 49). And yet: "My testimony is valid, even though I do bear witness about myself; because I know where I come from, and where I am going" (8:14).

The Son, then, as child, has his room for play, and as the wisdom of God he can "play in his presence continually, play throughout the wide earth" (Prov 8:30f.). But it is the Father's good pleasure that wholly fills this room for play, so that the Son always does what pleases the Father and "exactly fulfills his command" (Jn 14:31).

4

BECOMING GOD'S CHILDREN

WE MUST MARVEL when we realize the essential difference that carves out a gulf between the ordinary children of men and the Son of God who becomes a child: How could the children of Adam and Eve become children of God in the way that Jesus was the Son of the Father? We could understand how we men could be addressed, for his sake, as "children" by way of tenderness, in the way Paul calls his disciple and friend Timothy "my child" (2 Tim 2:1). At the limit we could also understand how the Father could "adopt" us men as his children out of love for his Son, by purchasing our freedom from slavery to the law (Gal 4:5) and, more deeply, by conferring on us that same "Spirit" that also animates his eternal Son (Rom 8:15). Once we look closer, however, we shall see that this "adoption" is nowhere understood as a mere juridical act: the

37

last doubt disappears when we hear that in this event we are no longer "born of any human blood, or by the will of the flesh or of the man, but of God himself" (Jn 1:13). And, in order that this inconceivable event should take place, God has given the eternal Son full authority to accomplish it (cf. Jn 1:12f.). God the Father empowers his Son to have us be begotten or born together with him from God. In his dialogue with Nicodemus, Jesus calls this "being born anew" or "from above" (Jn 3:3).

Such a thing becomes imaginable only if the Son of God unites us with himself through his Incarnation, only if he has first identified himself with us by means of the mysterious event we can describe as a "vicarious representation" or as a "pro-existence", that is, a being-for, an existence lived only on behalf of another. This occurred not only when "he took our sins upon himself" (Is 53:12 = 1 Jn 3:5), for this would simply remove our guilt. At a deeper level, it occurred when he assumed our entire person into himself and made a "new man" out of us (Eph 4:24; Col 3:10). And, although this is definitively accomplished at the Cross and in the Eucharist, this "being-in-him" is already contained in God's plan before the foundation of the world, for the Father "chose us *in him* before the world was founded, . . . and predestined us for sonship through Jesus Christ for him", the Father (Eph 1:4f.). Our carnal

38

birth indeed comes first within time (1 Cor 15:41), but its intentionality is already ordered to the second, definitive birth, so that it becomes "incorporated" into it (Eph 3:6). Here the expression "Body of Christ", used to describe the ecclesial community, is far more than a manner of speaking or a mere simile. It describes a total reality in which Christ is also portrayed as the Head and the other members together as the Body that belongs to him—an organism in which the Head no longer wants or is able to act in separation from his Body. And this occurred precisely when he gave his followers "full power to become children of God" (Jn 1:12), since he expressly made the Church participate in this act: "No one can enter the Kingdom of God without being born from water and Spirit" (Jn 3:5). Without doubt baptism is meant here, which introduces a person into the community of Christ's members by bestowing the divine Spirit of the Father and the Son: both things are inseparable, so that the children who are thus born receive God as Father and the Church as Mother at the baptismal font—the Church, in so far as she acts with Christ's authority: only in this manner are they taken up into the community of God's holy children, henceforth real brothers and sisters.

The original event is trinitarian: the Church is to baptize "in the name of the Father and of the Son and of the Holy Spirit" (Mt 28:19), since the baptized, together with Christ, become children of the Father. This is a filiation which the Son communicates to them and which is guaranteed by the reception of the Holy Spirit of God into their own spirit and heart. Instead of saying that the Son draws us into his own eternal birth from the bosom of the Father, the tradition of the Church often says that the Father begets his Son "into our hearts"; but this expression ("divine birth") conveys the same meaning as the first. On the basis of this inclusion of us in his sonship, the Risen Christ, after the completion of his whole work of vicarious representation, can call us his "brothers" (Jn 20:17).

This is an inconceivable grace, but it is also the highest kind of challenge; for now the Spirit of Christ calls out "Abba, Father!" (Gal 4:6; Rom 8:15) incessantly from our depths, and, as St. Paul continually insists, this exclamation must go hand in hand with our whole existence as children of God. This demands of us a continual repetition of what we already were in the mind of God "before the foundation of the world", but also a repetition of what we have lived, after our conception and birth, as "archetypical identity" in separation from our mother. What is called for is not at all a form of infantilism, but a repetition of the eternal Son's loving readiness to obey the "command" (*mandatum*) of the Father: we must persevere, together with Christ, in fleeing to the Father, in entrusting ourselves to the Father, in imploring and thanking the Father. The model for all of this is Christ at the highest point of his maturity and responsibility with regard to his mission. And the more we identify ourselves with the mission entrusted to us, in the manner of the eternal Son, the more thoroughly do we become sons and daughters of the Heavenly Father: the whole Sermon on the Mount testifies to this. In the figures of the great saints the truth is crystal clear: Christian childlikeness and Christian maturity are not in tension with one another. Even at an advanced age, the saints enjoy a marvelous youthfulness.

Here we could raise the question of the justification of infant baptism, but such a discussion would go beyond the limits of our meditation. Let us simply say this: the newborn child that is baptized is taken up at a fundamental level into the all-embracing and sheltering community of saints. Now this community does not exist outside of time, but reproduces itself in successive generations and, therefore, by its very nature, assumes the task of educating minors in Christian maturity. It would be unjust toward children to introduce them to Christian teaching and existence only as little pagans and catechumens, in order to leave it up to them to choose the Faith on their own responsibility at a point in time difficult to determine. For one thing, to attain to the very maturity in question they need the grace of baptism. Then, too, the Church, as a communion of faith, can by right impose on believers the responsibility of seeing to the education of children in a fully responsible faith. Nor ought we to forget that from his very origin the child possesses something like an incontrovertible faith-instinct, and this instinct provides an incalculable "capital" for the education of the child in Christian faith even after the separation in his consciousness between divine and human goodness. Finally, the Church does not dispense the sacrament of baptism in order to acquire for herself an increase in membership but in order to consecrate a human being to God and to communicate to that person the divine gift of birth from God. The Church has the competency to hand over a man to God and thus entrust him also to God's fatherly care. The extent of the precautions that must be taken in this matter can not be determined only by ordinances of the Church but also by the shared reflections of the parties concerned.

5

LIVING AS GOD'S CHILDREN

IT MAY BE THAT THIS Christian requirement to keep our divine childlikeness alive in all areas of our existence becomes more difficult the more technical man seeks to shape and govern everything on his own. Materialism is not alone in thinking that it can "redeem" man for itself through the dogma of atheism. Positivism, too, has the same intention, and *its* dogma forbids every truly philosophical question from being asked: it measures out the horizon of sensible thought solely on the basis of the surveyable "facts". The man who wants to attain to his puzzling origins and understand them can do this only by *making himself* as he proceeds, and we are decidedly making great strides along this road of the "makability of man". Nothing, compared to this, has ever more emptied the wondrous mystery of childhood of its value. But the ideal of man's self-fabrication is infallibly also his self-destruction: he becomes the Golem. And for this reason we may say that it is in our time that the contrasting Christian *leitmotiv* of birth from God—the childhood in God of even adult, active and inventive man—attains to its full and even increased validity.

We must now show the essential traits of the man who lives this childhood in God as an adult. These are most evident in Christ himself, since he retained all the traits of the child of God even as he was entrusted with the difficult, superhuman task of leading the whole world back home to God.

All his words and deeds reveal that he abides in looking up to the Father with eternal childlike amazement: "The Father is greater than I" (Jn 14:28). Indeed, he is irretrievably greater in so far as he is the origin of all things, even of the Son, and the Son never thinks of trying to "catch up" to this his Source: by so doing he would only destroy himself. He knows himself to be sheer Gift that is given to itself and which would not exist without the Giver who is distinct from the Gift and who nonetheless gives himself within it. What the Father gives is the capacity to be a self, freedom, and thus autonomy, but an autonomy which can be understood only as a surrender of self to the other. The phenomenon of Jesus shows the total unity existing between a freedom scandalous to the Jews—a freedom which even sets itself above their highest authority, the law, and relativizes this law with respect to its divine origin—and Jesus' abiding contemplation of the Father. "The Son can do nothing on his own initiative; he does only what he sees the Father doing, . . . for the Father loves the Son and shows him everything that he does" (Jn 5:19f.). Above the abstract law there is at work the concrete Spirit who is common to Father and Son and is the Spirit of freedom who enables the incarnate Son to know what is absolutely right in the deepest part of his freedom, that absolute right which radiates from the Father's unappealable freedom. But this highest good is handed over to the Son's innermost being ("I and the Father are one", Jn 10:30), for when the Father hands over everything to the Son this "everything" includes the Father's freedom. And precisely this handing-over is the object of infinite amazement, wonderment and gratitude. For the act whereby the Father eternally hands everything over to the Son is always in the present: it is never something concluded, in the past, belonging to a previous epoch, or something obligatory and owed which exists outside the free outpouring of love. Even if it is something remembered from time immemorial, it also remains something offered ever anew, something hoped for with all the infinite trust of love. We can be sure that the human Child Jesus was in amazement over everything: beginning with the existence of his loving Mother, then passing on to his own existence, finally going from both to all the forms offered by the surrounding world, from the tiniest flower to the boundless skies. But this amazement derives from the much deeper amazement of the eternal Child who, in the absolute Spirit of Love, marvels at Love itself as it permeates and transcends all that is. "The Father is greater": this comparative remains the locus where he abides since it signifies far more than the positive "great", but also much more that the superlative "the greatest", which would signal that an unsurpassable limit had been reached. The comparative is the linguistic form of amazement.

In the world of men, childlike amazement is not easy to preserve since so much in education aims at learning habits, mastering tasks and grasping automatic functions. Technology (think of all the electronic toys for children) only adds a new dimension to this delight in mastering things. But through all ages of life the interpersonal *thou* abides as an unmasterable reality, which from the Christian perspective, on the basis of the second part of the Great Commandment, remains an occasion for amazed awe at the freedom of the other, precisely because this freedom is to be approached only under the sign of love. As the erotic faculties of the growing person begin to blossom, the ability to marvel that was enjoyed at the dawn of life again awakens in the same primal sense. Now the Christian task lies in trying to deepen the erotic faculty from the surface of the senses into the depths of the heart: for here eros can keep alive an awed amazement at one's partner's self-surrender within all the routine of the common life, even after the first sensual stimulus has evaporated. But, for the person who is open to the absolute, there exists another kind of amazement with regard to nature as we know it outside ourselves. To be sure, the seed shoots up, spring returns again, and we take note of all the varieties of animals. But is it not amazing that all of this *is*? Is not the splendor of a flower or the imploring or grateful look of a dog just as amazing as the functioning of a new airplane (in which we admire more the inventive spirit of man than the pliancy of matter)?

"The Father is greater than I" lies hidden in all human experiences. God remains even in what he, the ever greater one, has handed over to his creatures as their own. No motion of love on the part of a created freedom, even in the case of a thing that has been given the ability to give itself, can ever be wrested by the receiver into his power.

This has a second direct consequence: the elemental thanksgiving, the model for which we again see in the eternal Child Jesus. Thanksgiving, in Greek *eucharistia*, is the quintessence of Jesus' stance toward the Father. "Father, I thank you for having heard me", he says at Lazarus' grave,

conscious that the Father has given him the power
to raise the dead (Jn 11:41). We witness the same
glance of imploring and thanksgiving toward
heaven on the occasion of the multiplication of
the loaves (Mk 6:41 and par.), which is a prelude
to the definitive Eucharist. On this latter occasion
he distributes the bread and the wine only after
having given thanks to the Father who allows him
to accomplish this pouring-out of himself (Mk
14:23; Mt 26:27; Lk 22:17, 19; 1 Cor 11:24). The
most decisive act of thanksgiving by Jesus takes
place precisely here, at the moment when he gives
himself away, and this is something that should
remain present to all who utter the word Eucharist. Every eucharistic celebration by the ecclesial
community is in essence an act of thanksgiving
to the Father during which all participants, together with the Son, give thanks for the "Great
Banquet" in which they not only participate but
by virtue of which they are enabled to give themselves away together with the Son. In almost
countless passages, Paul reminds his communities
of this need to give thanks to God, and just as
often he himself thanks God for having received
the grace that enables him to spend himself for
Christ's work: "Thanking the Father for having
enabled us to . . ." (Col 1:12), and this "incessantly" (1 Thes 2:13).

In everything the human child is dependent on
free acts of giving by others: in him, plea and

thanks are still indistinguishably one. Because he is needy he is also thankful in his deepest being, before making any free, moral decision to be so. And when he grows older and we say to him "Say *please*", "say *thank you*", we are not teaching him anything new but only trying to bring into his more conscious sphere what is already present from the beginning. He should not be taught to be thankful only for specific things received, but his original awareness that he himself—his "I"—is something given and that he must give thanks for it, should be also transposed into the sphere of the maturing consciousness. To be a child means to owe one's existence to another, and even in our adult life we never quite reach the point where we no longer have to give thanks for being the person we are. This means that we never quite outgrow our condition of children, nor do we therefore ever outgrow the obligation to give thanks for ourselves or to continue to ask for our being. Individual men, cultures and institutions may forget this. Only the Christian religion, which in its essence is communicated by the eternal child of God, keeps alive in its believers the lifelong awareness of their being children, and therefore of having to ask and give thanks for things. Jesus does not insist on this childlike "say *please*", "say *thank you*", because otherwise the gifts would be refused, but in order that they may be recognized as gifts. "Ask and it shall be given to you; seek and you shall find; knock and it shall be opened to you" (Mt 7:7), and this with such certainty that "even as you ask you can already give thanks for what you have received" (Mk 11:24).

Here we see the source of the prohibition in the Sermon on the Mount against worrying about the morrow, and of the request in the Our Father that asks only for today's bread. Such things are understandable only coming from the children of God, for, when children ask for something, they always do so in the emphatic present, and when they sit down at a full table they never think of tomorrow's meal. Adults, who have to provide for themselves and for their children, have no alternative but to worry in advance. Jesus also tells the parable of the "steward of unjust mammon" (Lk 16:1–7), who is fired by the proprietor and who reflects on what he will do after his dismissal: "I know what I must do, to make sure that, when I am let go from my stewardship, there will be people who give me house and home" (16:4). Jesus praises him, but only with regard to his worldly "wisdom", which is greater than that of the "sons of light". For these, however, the foresight is not to be that of the world. The advice "Become friends with unjust mammon so that, when it is a thing of the past, you may be received into the eternal dwelling-place" (Lk 16:9) really means: Give to the poor what is yours so that, doing so, you may store up for yourselves "a treasure in heaven" (Mt 19:21). This too is a childlike attitude, since children are always ready to give and offer the necessary counterpart to those who vainly seek to provide for the morrow. Jesus does not draft an order of society in which rich countries come to the support of poor countries; rather, he outlines a community in which those who have, come to the aid of those who lack, and into this community he introduces himself as the ultimate criterion for a genuine childlike attitude: "I was hungry, thirsty, a stranger, naked, sick, in prison", and you either gave to me or did not give to me, you behaved like prodigal children or like greedy adults, and in the end it is by this that you shall be judged (Mt 25:37–46). Childlike carefreeness and childlike joy in giving complete one another in the vision of humanity of this big Child of the Father.

A third reality which the childlike attitude of Christian life keeps alive is the intimate character of the Church as mystery. To be sure, there is an aspect of brotherhood that permeates the Church, in keeping with Jesus' emphasis on all of us being brothers, which is the reason no one of us should call himself father or teacher, "For one alone is your father: the Father in heaven", and "one is your Teacher, Christ" (Mt 23:8–10). Such brotherhood, then, obtains for all only under the common Father and Teacher. But he, moreover, without annulling this brotherhood, has delegated his office as teacher for the building up of the Church: "He who hears you, hears me" (Lk 10:16), and in him, who is the Divine Word, the Father is heard as well. Here we discover a new sphere for the exercise of Christian childlikeness: in the ecclesial reception of the sacraments authorized by Christ, in the proclamation of his Word and in the leadership ordained by him. This is most evident with the sacraments. God alone prepares in the Church the great banquet of the Eucharist, to which we are invited as his children. He alone confers forgiveness of sins and the Holy Spirit in a sacrament. He alone takes a matrimonial promise of fidelity up into the indissolubility of the nuptial covenant between Christ and his Church. He alone consecrates a man to the fullness of sacramental powers or in the surrender of his life through definitive vows. Anyone acceding to a sacrament is a pure childlike receiver, even if he must contribute something of his own, but this something is nothing other than the perfect readiness of a child. When listening to a sermon, the Christian must in essence be animated by this same attitude of childlike receptivity, for who could presume to argue with God's Word? Here, however, the receiver is in a position of distinguishing what in the sermon or other instruction is the Word of God and what is merely human words obscuring God's Word: he can make this distinction by virtue of the Holy Spirit that he personally has received. But, in the presence of God's Word, we all remain children who cannot understand everything to the root; we must, therefore, beware of setting up our own lack of understanding as the objective limit in the reception of the proclaimed doctrine. At school, children continually have things to learn that they do not yet know. We must remember this also with regard to the Church's pastoral office: the biblical image of the sheep that are led to pasture does not indicate immaturity, but rather the docility of even mature Christians. Such tractability in the following of Christ himself must be more intrinsic than any criticism directed at a more peripheral aspect in the style of leadership in the Church. For, despite all human imperfection, the person entrusted with the burden of leadership is the first to obey with a simple obedience: "Feed my sheep" (Jn 21:17), and do it "not as someone who rules it over your community, but as a model for the flock" (1 Pet 5:3). Only in the light of the docility and obedience of the eternal Son can the Christian defend himself against the charge that he is treated as a minor in his Church. And it is also with this reference that he must overcome the perennial temptation to confuse the brotherhood of the Church with a worldly democracy.

A fourth and last point. The child has time to take time as it comes, one day at a time, calmly, without advance planning or greedy hoarding of time. Time to play, time to sleep. He knows nothing of appointment books in which every moment has already been sold in advance. When Paul exhorts us to "buy up the time" (Col 4:5; Eph 5:16) he probably means precisely the opposite, that is, that we ought not to squander hours and days like cheap merchandise but that we should live the time that is given us now, in all its fullness: but the point is neither to "enjoy it to the full" nor to "make the most of it", but only that we should receive with gratitude the full cup that is handed to us. The moment is full because in it all of time is gathered up, effortlessly as it were. The present moment contains the memory of already having received as much as the hope of receiving time now. This is why the child is not afraid at the fleetingness of the present moment: stopping to consider it would hinder us from accepting the moment in its fullness, would keep us from "buying it up", from ransoming it.

Play is possible only within time so conceived, and also the unresisting welcome we give to sleep. And only with time of this quality can the Christian find God in all things, just as Christ found the Father in all things. Pressured man on the run is always postponing his encounter with God to a "free moment" or a "time of prayer" that must constantly be rescheduled, a time that he must laboriously wrest from his overburdened workday. A child that knows God can find him at every moment because every moment opens up for him and shows him the very ground of time: as if it reposed on eternity itself. And this eternity, without undergoing change, walks hand in hand for the child with transitory time. God defines himself as "I am who I am", which also means: My being is such that I shall always be present in every moment of becoming.

6

TO BE A CHILD ABOVE ALL

IN THE CENTER OF THE CHRISTIAN RELIGION, looming high, many see the Cross. From the first graffiti scratched on walls as a mockery to Christians, through all the great styles of Christian art, the Cross stands as the central symbol for faith in Jesus Christ. Whether as Constantine's triumphal cross or, as at Ravenna, as radiant cross of the resurrection, or yet again as Gothic cross of sorrows, in all its forms there lies behind the distinctive mark of the Christian a frightful historical crime, a manner of torture of which Cicero says it represents "the most cruel and repulsive of all agonies" to which a man can be subjected (*In Verr.* II, 5). And it is to the Cross that the Christian is challenged to follow his Master: no path of redemption can make a detour around it. "Whoever does not daily take up his cross" (Lk 9:23) cannot be Jesus' disciple.

On the other hand, we know that Jesus' suffering on the Cross was redemptive solely because, as eternal Son of God, he could represent humanity as a whole before the Father and atone for it. Hence, in his discipleship, renunciation or suffering can make sense and bear fruit only because the sufferer has first been made into a child of God by the eternal Son.

If we open up St. John's prologue, we notice that it nowhere speaks about the Cross, but rather about the Word, God's Son, being in God from all eternity, about his being the creating Light and Life of the world, about his assuming human flesh and giving those who receive him the power of being born from God, that is, the power of becoming children of God together with him. The Word of God is expressly said to be the only-begotten Son who, beyond the Mosaic law, shows us the "glorious splendor" of the Father and bestows on us "grace upon grace", the "plenitude" of "grace and truth". In this way he has "explained" to us the God who is hidden to all as the only one who knows him out of an eternal experience— "explained" him not exteriorly as a teacher teaches his students, but through the interior participation in his own status as child (Jn 1:1–18).

The prologue of the Letter to the Ephesians, which we have already quoted, portrays for us God's original plan of salvation. We are exhorted to begin everything by blessing and praising God, "the Father of our Lord Jesus Christ, who has bestowed on us in Christ every spiritual blessing in the heavenly realms. In Christ he chose us before the world was founded, to be set apart in holiness, to be without blemish in his sight. In his love he destined us—such was his will and pleasure—to be accepted as his sons through Jesus Christ, in order that the glory of his gracious gift, so graciously bestowed on us in his Beloved, might redound to his praise" (Eph 1:3–6). Such is the first purpose of creation: our being children in the only Son, that the Father and the children might reciprocally bless one another. Only in order to reach this goal is the means then named in the following verse: "the redemption through his blood, the forgiveness of sins by virtue of the richness of his grace" (1:7).

And the prologue of the Letter to the Hebrews, which will deal mostly with Christ's character as high priest, likewise begins with the culmination of all partial revelations of God in his all-embracing uttering of himself in the Son who is established as total heir of the world. To this Son the highest attributes are ascribed: he is "the radiance of the glory" of God, "the stamp of God's very being". His superiority to the angels is described in detail, for these are all "but ministering spirits, sent out to serve, for the sake of those who are to inherit salvation". And if the eternal Son accomplishes his work of salvation for us, it is in order to present us before the Father along with himself: "Behold, here we are, I and the children that God has given to me." The difference between him who is eternally begotten of the Father and us who are created into the bosom of time is, as it were, overlooked, and along with it also the difference between "him who makes holy and those who are made holy", for "God, through whom and for whom everything is, has willed to lead all his sons to glory. . . . The sanctifier and the sanctified do, indeed, all proceed from the same One [from the Father], and therefore he [the Son] is not ashamed to call them his brothers" (Heb 1–2).

Still other introductions in the New Testament strike the same tone: the Letter to the Colossians, the two Letters of Peter, the great Letter of John. Everywhere the theme which is launched immediately and in detail is the redemption through the sufferings of the Son. But everything concerning the form of the redemption—both Jesus' sufferings "that pave the way" (Heb 12:2) and our following of him—belongs to the road leading to the goal, and is a means to the end. And only because Christ is above all the eternal Son can he achieve the deed of salvation and, through it, make us sons. What is more—and this is something Christians often forget—only because and in so far as they are sons and daughters of the Father does their suffering, their life's struggle and their

dying have co-redemptive value. The many sufferings that Paul tells us he had to undergo were
all suffered "in Christ", by a member of his Mys-
tical Body, in order to participate in the "holy
exchange" that occurred on the Cross: "We always
bear the sufferings of Jesus' death in our body",
so that, "just as death is at work in us, life may
be at work in you" (2 Cor 4:10, 12).

Jesus, thus, suffers as the Son. In his own prayer,
the child's word "Abba!" ("Papa") is first heard
on the Mount of Olives (Mk 14:36). Even though
the Father can now no longer respond, still all
Jesus' suffering—even to the cry of abandonment
on the Cross—is suffered in the spirit of childhood. And after the Son, like a lost child in an
eerie forest, has been led through all the horrors
of Holy Saturday, he can proclaim triumphantly
on Easter Day: "I go up to my Father and your
Father" (Jn 20:17), for he has finally accomplished
it: his own have now become sons together with
him; they have been "raised up together with him
and, together with him, they have been transferred
to heaven" (Eph 2:6).

Thus, beyond the abiding reverential distance
between him, our "Lord and Master" (Jn 13:13),
and us, there also exists a certain equality before
the Father which enables us to do in the Church
what he does with us: we may present him to the
Father on our own behalf, just as he presents us
to the Father. He himself wills this when he gives

us the authority communicated in the command: "Do this in memory of me." So it is that the Church dares to present him to the Father as a guarantor for humanity: "Look with favor on your Church's offering, and see the Victim whose death has reconciled us to yourself. . . . May this sacrifice which has made our peace with you, advance the peace and salvation of all the world" (Third Eucharistic Prayer). Since Christ gave his own sacrifice to the Church, this offering becomes for the Church herself a sacrificial gift brought before the Father: ". . . From the many gifts you have given us, we offer to you, God of glory and majesty, this holy and perfect sacrifice. . . . Look with favor on these offerings and accept them as once you accepted the gifts of your servant Abel, the sacrifice of Abraham, our Father in faith . . ." (First Eucharistic Prayer). Christ could have given us, his brothers, nothing more precious than this to offer to the Father, and this "so that from east to west a perfect offering may be made to the glory of your name" (Third Eucharistic Prayer). With confidence, and without arrogance, we are entitled to speak as an ecclesial community, and say: "Lord, look upon this sacrifice which you have given to your Church; and by your Holy Spirit, gather all who share this bread and wine into the one body of Christ, a living sacrifice of praise" (Fourth Eucharistic Prayer).

The hands of the Church hold the eternal Child up toward the eternal Father, in order that, at first, the Father may see only him, but so that then, in this one Child, he may see all the other children which the Child takes with him so as not to appear alone before the Father.

But then we must also consider something like the complementary reverse. At the end of his farewell discourse, Jesus says: "When that day comes you will make your request in my name, and I do not say that I shall pray to the Father for you, for the Father loves you himself" (Jn 16:26). Here it is the eternal Child who holds us up to the Father, no longer now as the "pioneer" and "mediator" who is our spokesman before the Father, but, in a way, as one who stands behind us (his work of mediation is finished) exposing us to the full brunt of the Father's love. If, in the first instance, the Church as priestess offers up the Son to the Father, now it is the Son as "eternal high priest" who offers us up to the Father.

All of this, to be sure, contains the highest kind of dramatic earnestness; and yet, at the same time, it is a kind of heavenly game in which all the variations of divine love are played out by the children of God. In this game, or play, it becomes clear that the whole tragedy of the Cross, and everything that belongs to Christ's high-priesthood and to both the common and the special priesthood of the faithful, possesses its permanent foundation in God's triune mystery of childhood.

To be a Child of the Father, then, holds primacy over the whole drama of salvation, since it is what leads the Son of God from his human childhood through his public ministry and rejection by man all the way to his high-priestly office on the Cross. That same reality of being the Father's Child is what takes the Church, born herself as a child from the wound in Christ's side, up into a consenting realization of the priestly mystery of the Cross which is continually renewed in the Church's daily life and Eucharist. This primacy of trinitarian Childhood over the work of redemption clearly signifies that the total redemptive deed with its emphatically "adult" earnestness can, in the last analysis, be accomplished only by virtue of the childlike stance of the God-Man and within the childlike faith of his bride, the Church. Much as we are to look for the presence of the Father in the Son ("Whoever sees me, sees the Father"), this is far from implying that the figure and face of the Son thereby vanish. On the contrary! Even if the prophet ascribes to the Child Messiah the name "eternal father" (Is 9:5) and it is he who, in a certain way, is to be looked upon as the begetter of his Church and all her saving power within the world's history, nevertheless he in no manner comes to substitute for his Father but rather represents unsurpassably for us the Father's paternal

64

qualities. In so far as she is our Mother, the Church ought never to lose this from sight: no girl is born a mother; no motherhood falls ready-made from heaven. And, therefore, the Church's motherhood, wrought by grace, rests upon the primary foundation of her own childhood, which persists unforgettably. This should be kept before our eyes as we now pass, in conclusion, to consider the indispensable Mother of the Child Jesus.

THE MOTHER, A FRUITFUL CHILD

MANY LEGENDS THRIVE all about the childhood of Mary, about which we know nothing. The most famous is that concerning her entry into the temple, where she went to be wholly consecrated to God as a temple virgin. But we do not really need this external event, for faith assures us that Mary came into existence already as one expressly consecrated to God, and that at every moment of her life she, alone of mankind, remained "immaculately holy" as one chosen by God in his eternal plan of salvation for all men (Eph 1:4). We say "alone of all men", because within this plan she held a special place: she was to be the cooperating cause of the incarnation of the Redeemer of all others and, in so far as he became a human child, she was also to be a human model for him. And, further, she could not have been these things if she had been deprived of the

Holy Spirit's instruction and had known nothing of the Son's eternal Childhood in the Father's bosom. As his Mother, she had to instruct the temporal Child about whom the Holy Spirit had instructed her in advance that he was the Child of God.

Like no other creature, therefore, she was initiated into all the mysteries of being a child; yet the unheard-of but essential thing about her was that she could not outgrow this condition of being a child of God even as she continued to mature physically and spiritually. Regardless of how her relationship to her earthly parents may have changed during her process of maturing, given that the shadow of original sin did not fall upon her we know that her childlike relationship to God could not have been troubled by those changes. Consequently, under the guidance of God's grace, she was enabled, while remaining a child, to bear maternal fruit and, as a mother, to remain inviolately childlike.

Already at this point we must extend our field of vision to the Cross, standing under which Mary will be designated by her Son as the Mother-Church ("Behold your son!"). Nor must we forget that, even as the archetypical Church, she will continue to bear the same childlike traits she possessed from the beginning and without which she could not form Christians by sacrament and doctrine into children of God.

Everything begins with the young woman who is termed Mother of the "Son of the Most High" by the angel bringing her God's greeting. Mary thus learns that the Most High has ever borne a Son in his bosom, and that this Son has now chosen her bosom as dwelling-place. If she were to reflect on her own possibilities aided by an ordinary "adult" understanding, the result of her meditation would simply be: "impossible". What proportion could there be between the bosom of God and a dark and narrow human bosom? However, being perfect child of God, she does not reflect upon herself but places herself at the disposal of God's every action, precisely from her distance as the "lowly servant" upon whom the Lord has deigned to lay his eyes (Lk 1:48). "Behold, I am the Lord's handmaid. Let it be done to me according to his word": such a statement presupposes a pure childlike attitude that entrusts everything to the Father, even when he wills to interfere in her relationship with Joseph, to whom she is engaged.

In what results from this assent there becomes visible for the first time in God's story with man something extraordinary, and a perfect archetype: the spontaneously trusting child's word—which expects everything from the heavenly Father and is spoken with untrammeled freedom—at once makes fruitful the Word of God implanted within itself, the Word of God which is God's eternal

Child. This could not be seen in the Old Testament, where bodily fruitfulness still presupposed an adult body and spirit; nor could it be seen even in Jesus' parables, since these still used the examples of ordinary human situations ("A man had two sons . . ."). But what comes into evidence in Mary for the first time will henceforth remain a real possibility in Christ's Church: the fruitfulness of the child, who, without regard for the fullness of sexual maturity, can bear fruit for God out of the total unity of her body and soul. For this, the only condition required is that one be open to God to the very bottom of one's being.

But a child must go to school. And so Mary is taken into rigorous instruction by the Holy Spirit during the time of her pregnancy.

It is not her body that must learn motherhood; it is her whole person that must learn what one is to be and do as Mother of God. As the Immaculate One, she has always had the Spirit inside her, for she could never have learned what was necessary by means of exterior instruction. She will have to do both things at once: introduce her Child into the business of being human (and this does not merely mean teaching him how to walk and speak, but also introducing him to the religion of his fathers) and learn steadily more from her Child how one behaves as a child of God. There was already much to be learned during the pregnancy: how to overcome motherly fears, how to rise to the occasion of such a birth and of the unimaginable motherly tasks connected with such a Child. Some inkling must also have been present that the Child, too, would be precipitated into an abyss of fears and sorrows. Will the Mother, separated from her Child, be equal to these experiences? And if the Child is really to be "Son of the Most High", how will he, bearer of such a divine and human task, behave toward her, poor handmaid of the Lord? Question upon question that cannot be solved in advance, but which will have to be taken to the school of the Holy Spirit and let stand as questions—questions to be borne. . . . The education of a child of God by the Holy Spirit is never completed.

The Mother's long period of life with her growing Son is, for the Mother, a life in faith. She does not see the God in him; only from afar does she suspect his particular relationship to the Father. She does not understand what the twelve-year-old says to her. And, left behind with the unbelieving "brothers", how much will she understand about his public actions? The Son shall leave her behind and hardly acknowledge her any more: "Woman, what is there between us?" When she wants to visit him, he is so busy with his new family that he has no time for her. When a woman from the crowd calls her blessed, she is pushed back into the anonymity of the crowd: "Indeed, blessed are those who hear the word of God and keep it." On the one hand, she is held up as the very model for the new faith; on the other hand, as a representative of purely biological origins, she is relegated to an archaic past that has been surpassed. All of this is now the school of the Son, her training in his own abandonment, in which she will receive her share under the Cross.

When speaking of this participation by Mary in the Son's separation from the Father during the Passion—a separation so necessary to salvation history—one is accustomed to referring only to her virginal motherhood. This is quite correct. But we should also consider that this unique distinction of Mary's has its deepest basis in her equally unique status as child of God, and that this divine childhood of hers itself has its model in the Son's own eternal status as Child. This, in turn, points us again in the direction of the unity particularly explored by St. John: the unity between the abiding dependency of the Son on the Father ("My teaching is not mine", Jn 7:16) and the autonomously responsible mission which the Father entrusts to the Son, the unity, if you will, between being a child and being an adult. When Christians pray to Jesus through Mary, they must necessarily allow themselves to be initiated by Mary's model into the Son's unique stance as Child. For, when a Christian allows himself successfully to be led by Jesus into the Father's bosom, this process already includes from the outset Mary's childlike relationship to the Father in the Holy Spirit.

This does not change when Mary (who is simply called "woman" in John) comes under the Cross as bride to stand by the new Adam, when, in her human way, she cooperates through her assent in having the Church emerge from her own sword-pierced heart, as well as from her Son's. Bound to the Disciple as her new son, she is not only the maternal figure of the Church that gives birth to all the other members of the Body after it has borne the Head (Rev 12:17), and remains their Mother; she is also the archetypical member of this Church, who in all her members participates, through Christ and by virtue of word and sacrament, in the grace of being a child in the bosom of the Father. As was already said at the beginning of these meditations, all forms of the following of Christ within the Marian Church by carrying Christ's Cross with him, all priestly functions of the hierarchy and of the laity, are in the end ordered to this highest grace of childhood. In the figure of Mary all Christians can see that this childhood in God—which is the locus of fruitfulness received from the Source—can be one thing, even in the world of men, with the fruitfulness worked by grace.

This results in one last thing. In the Apocalypse the Woman who, with great pain, gives birth to the Messiah between heaven and earth, doubtless also bears all the sorrows of Israel, the people which is to bear its Messiah from its simultaneously believing and sinful womb. If Israel had not been so unfaithful to its God, so much pain and sorrow would not have been required. And yet the faith of Abraham and the fidelity of the prophets are very much there as realities which cannot fail but participate in the birth of the Redeemer. But how is this mixed theological heritage to be housed within the destiny of the modest and innocent Maiden of Nazareth? Only by seeing that the election of the Virgin to be Mother of the Redeemer antedated every other aspect of her mission. Her Son first had to be the Child of the Father in order then to become man and be capable of taking up on his shoulders the burden of a guilty world. In the same way, too, the Mother had to be the first thought in God's plan of salvation, so that she could then become, like her Son, the bearer of all the constellations of salvation history. The promise made to the woman upon her expulsion from paradise—that her issue would trample the head of the serpent (Gen 3:15)— already hints at this darkly. But we see it quite clearly in Mary's encounter with Elizabeth, when the younger, Messianic Child blesses the older child, his forerunner, in his mother's womb, thus blessing all Old Testament prophecy as well. The Last is, in God's plans, the First, that for whose sake everything that precedes has existed. And so the child Mary, chosen to be the Mother of the eternal Child, is what gives meaning to everything that occurs from Adam and Abraham onward, up to herself, everything entrusted to her atoning perfection within the work of her Son.